Women of Purpose, Power and Prosperity

*Powerful Stories of Women Who Moved from Pain to Walk
in Their Purpose and Prosperity*

VOLUME 1 | I Made It Anyway

Presented by

Pastor Veda A. McCoy

Forward by Rev. Dr. Kellie V. Hayes

Dedication

This book is dedicated to my mother, the late Minister Irene B. Nicely. Thank you for showing me that pain does not have the final say and that purpose is available to us all, no matter where you begin.

I also dedicated this book to my mother in love, Rev. Dr. Odessa McCoy and my two godmothers, Lady M. Owens and Dr. Patricia Ross, who have all loved and nurtured me. Thank you for showing me how to keep purpose in view and paving the road to my destiny with lots of unconditional love, patience and support.

****

Thank You Sentiments from Pastor Veda

Thank you to my husband, Overseer Marvin E. McCoy who has been my greatest source of strength for nearly forty years.

To children, Marvin Myer and Johntae Marvyce, you are purpose and passion personified. Thank you for allowing me to be your mom and giving me so many chances to try and try again.

To my executive and administrative team, thank you for keeping me organized and making me look good! May the promise of Ephesians 6:8 rest upon your lives in manifold proportions!

To God be All the Glory!

Forward

**Women of Purpose, Power and Prosperity
Stories of Women who Moved from Pain to Discover their
Purpose to Walk in Power and Prosperity.**

Have you ever known you needed something, but didn't know what it was until it presented itself? I have, and with this book, *Women of Purpose, Power and Prosperity,* Pastor Veda McCoy and her co-authors have met a need in my life. Although I shouldn't be surprised, my friend Pastor Veda McCoy has a way of stepping into the divine intention of God and manifesting just what women need just at the right time. So I'm sure I'm not the only one who needed to be reminded in these precarious times that your dark and painful seasons don't define you, they refine you—if you let them. With the proper nurturing and wisdom, those seasons can unlock courage, strength and purpose. That is the core of Pastor Veda's heart for women, that we would all live an unlocked life! It doesn't matter if it is a prophetic institute or prayer breakfast, a tea, a special time of prayer and impartation, or a virtual conference providing the atmosphere for women to just breathe again. The point is your life is not over; it's just beginning. Surrender to the Spirit of God and unlock all of the hidden treasures within you that the world needs.

Just in case you may think unlocked living is for other women and not you, I want you to know that through this gift of God that you are holding in your hands you will discover that you too can live through pain, discover your unique purpose and use it to bring prosperity to yourself, your family and community. This is your answered prayer to remind you that God is no respecter of person, we overcome by the blood of the lamb and the word of our testimony. Receive the stories of these courageous women.

Rev. Dr. Kellie V. Hayes
Executive Pastor of Real Power A.M.E. Church
CEO of Enlightened Woman Enterprises

Table of Contents

Living for
The Love
of You

By Yolanda Chinn

Trust in God they say, Lord I have no other choice but to trust you. That's all I can do.

Walk through the doors of change! I realized I've been sitting at the doorsteps of change for four years. I had to ask myself, how long are you planning to sit still at this threshold? Especially when the doors are wide open for you. Honestly, I was scared. No, petrified. I was so used to knowing my little world, or at least that's what I felt and told myself. All familiar places and faces. I became so used to just knowing where to go, who to be with and most importantly what to do. It was always so plain and simple. Then the next thing I knew, the unknown entered my little world full speed ahead and I couldn't stop it. I couldn't even catch up. It happened so fast. Everything I knew and much of what I loved became threatened. You see it was a threat to me feeling so out of control. What's about to happen? What will it look like? What will it feel like? What will it take?

My two biggest supporters passed away within 5 months of each other. My mommy first, and then my husband. You couldn't have told me I'd become motherless and a young widow in a matter of months. I didn't know it at the time, but God showed me that I was an example to people on how to grieve as God would desire. I had lost other parents before, my paternal dad, father-in-law, and the only male in my life that never let me down, at least in my eyes, my dearest grand-daddy. He was definitely one of my "rocks" and a great supporter but when he passed away, I still had them. I still had my mommy and my husband. When they passed away, this was different. My two book ends were gone. It was as if I was a book on the shelf left to just lay down. No bookends to stand me up. Laying there feeling almost dead myself. I felt alone and my little world as I knew it was shattered into little bitty pieces. I didn't know how to pick the pieces up and quite frankly I didn't even care to put it back together without them here with me. There were days upon days that I felt so lost. Yet, I needed to be strong for my loving son. God gave me enough strength to want to live, for my son, for me, but most importantly for Him. Nothing, nothing seemed the same, and I kept telling myself that's because everything is so very different. It's crazy how all of the stuff they owned was still here. Their belongings remained in the same places where they left them behind and yet, those same belongings looked so different to me now. Almost unrecognizable but familiarly different.

I wished I had lived each day like it was their last, instead of bracing myself for THE last day. I probably would have included more kisses, some more talks etc. instead I spent most of the time caring for them in hopes to prolong their time. So not in my control. It never was. Ugh! I remember repeatedly saying, "I don't want to be doom and gloom." I thought I could control grief. I thought I could dictate or manipulate my grief, I had planned to tell it when to cry, when to stop, and when to be done and over. I certainly was wrong. I had to begin to just let the emotions happen as they came, release the cry, meditate and pray. Just as I loved my dear sweet loved ones, I needed to pour that same love into me. I was desperate to pour the pain of my losses into my purpose. I did so by keeping in touch with positive influences, counseling and prayer. I rediscovered myself and realized that I can live for the love of me while still loving them. I had it all wrong, I thought if I loved me and or anyone else, I'd lose or stop loving them. The more I began to live for the love of me, the more at peace I felt with God and myself. After all, I had no control over their lives or deaths. I knew it was God, and yet I still loved Him, so why not love me?

The Bible says God gives us the peace that surpasses all of our understanding. I had to run into the arms of Jesus, seeking that type of peace and joy. I found it. Yes, I found it right there, in the arms of Jesus. The strength during that time I had is unexplainable. I know for sure that it was from God. It was a result of answered prayers. You see, every time people prayed for me, their prayers always included strength. I can remember thinking to myself everyone keeps praying for my strength. Perhaps we just say it when we pray for folks. I didn't realize that I would definitely need that strength in so many ways. I don't take that lightly at all. I now know the true meaning of praying for strength and the need for it. Thank you Lord!

Once I received their diagnosis/prognosis, I wanted to give them as much as I could for the time they had. It was no time for regrets – only quality time mattered now. Every moment…every second counted. Everything and I mean everything was suddenly so different. The lessons I learned from them are so many. Like, how you handle hard circumstances and just being thankful for the opportunities you have are two lessons they taught me. Ironically, in the face of their deaths, they really showed me and others how to live. All I wanted to do for both of them was to live up to their standards, live for their love. I wanted to comfort them, love them, love them so hard that they'd be healed as if I had the power. Ha! Ain't it funny, how just when you think you're doing something God shows you a whole different way. Yep, the presence of God was all over this and once I realized it, I was mighty glad. I could feel God's presence every step of the way and I had to deal with it in a way I knew God would be pleased with. Trust me, this was not easy at all. This meant I now had to be very sure that my own feelings and intensions were out of the way. God was with me and he showed me he's been with me all the time. Deep down inside I knew it, but I began to believe it in an experienced way. This time I experienced it for myself, not just what I believed or what I was told. I saw it, felt it, the presence of God. Thus, the strength I needed to take care of them, and handle the new way of life for me, without them.

Losing them and finding me was not an easy process. Yet, I had to fight through the fears of living without them. It was not just the milestone times, or special occasions that were the hardest. It was the everyday living, like getting out of bed, laundry, house and car maintenance, grocery shopping and cooking. These were simple things we tend to take for granted, and now I was scared to do. There were so many daily simple things that I avoided, because it only amplified that they were no longer here and I was left behind to do them now for myself. I felt so forced into these changes. I realized that is was nothing but fear that was stopping me. I wasn't sure that I could do it, because before I had them to do it either for me or with me. Once I finally began to pick up the pieces and move forward with these simple things, remarkably I surprised myself, I can remember when I finally bought a new cell phone, it was a triumphant moment, a turning point and I felt relieved that "I can do it." I'm able to do these routine chores like everyone else. That's when I knew it was time to allow Loni to live beyond the bookends.

My mother and my husband were such beautiful people, that during my time of care taking and ultimate grief, there was so much laughter and love. Before I knew it, I could see the joy that they brought to their lives, our lives. As folks gathered during visits, and thereafter, so many memories were shared.

I'm very thankful for the support and love I received during the time of care taking and grief. Quite frankly, grateful for the love and support I still receive. Again, it is a testament to my loved ones lives, what they poured into others came back to us during the most critical times in need. So many faces all around, lots of hugs and teary eyes. I can see them fighting it, holding back the tears for my sake. I was able to hold on to them, treasure them and some of the stories I imagined I was there with them, just as if I lived those stories. I admit, I enjoyed the stories shared because it made me feel my loved ones' warmth. It was as if each story hugged me like a blanket as I clung on to each word. One word at a time hugged me so tight, I was able to be at peace knowing they were here, once with them and now again with me.

I found myself speaking to the Lord more and more out loud. It was like me saying, "Are you there, God? It's me, Loni." Just like Margaret, in my favorite childhood book by Judy Blume, titled *Are You There, God? It's Me, Margaret*. Every day I awaken I thank God, talk to him and ask of Him- "Lord, help me." Every day, I remind myself, I know I can only bring them with me as memories into my future. They will not be there, however, their spirits live on within me. I hear God say to me, turn the page Loni, walk in your new chapter of your life. When you turn the page, you'll see the next chapter, all you need to do is turn the page. It's time!

Move on…Nothing stays the same, can't you see that the atmosphere has changed?

Some say life is like a box of chocolates; I say it's a book. And each day that you awake, there is a new page to turn. So be thankful you have an opportunity to turn the page, now embrace the new page and walk in it. I know, sometimes it's hard, especially for those of us that love to remain in the past. It's hard to let go. It's ok to reminisce, but be careful don't stay stuck in the past. You already know that story, the pages before, yes you know them well, you've lived it. There's no need to rehearse them. As you grow, so do the chapters of your book. Be excited about what's on the next page. Page after page of each chapter will lead to fresh new ideas, experiences, growth, trials and triumphs! You ready? Turn the page with me and author another chapter…one day at a time.

Be your own "Change Agent!" Change is necessary, and sometimes it's a forced change beyond your control but once you turn that corner, turning the pages gets you closer to living for the love of you.

Forgiving The Unforgivable

Evangelist Trgina Hunter

My earliest viable memory is of me at age 3, watching my father throw my mother and my toys out of our home after a fight between him and my mother. Yes, my earliest memory is of my father demonstrating what I would eventually resolve to be his lack of love for me. So began my life-long journey of trying to figure out the ONE THING that would make my father love me.

I was a decent kid. I excelled in my schooling. Dad was in the Air Force; I was in Air Force JROTC. I even took JROTC in summer school for two years, and by the time I graduated HS, I out-ranked the battalion commander. Surely, ONE of my many accomplishments would make him love me...or so I thought. My father was the coolest man alive in my eyes, and I loved him with my everything. Because he couldn't demonstrate his love to me tangibly, I resolved that my father didn't love me, even though he was very present in my life.

I "became a woman" at 9. Around this same time, my mother met and married the creepiest man I'd ever met. From day one, his presence so completely upset my spirit it was palpable. Unfortunately, everyone just assumed that I didn't like him because he wasn't my father--as if my father was the shining example of fatherhood every man should follow. Within months of the wedding, my stepfather moved us out to Centreville, VA. Away from my family, away from my dad, away from my security, my place of peace. I was separated and secluded. My mother worked 2 jobs, so I was home alone with him a lot. A LOT. I went from being the little girl who didn't feel loved by her father to an adolescent being molested by her stepfather. For a long time, I didn't know what he was doing was wrong. My father didn't demonstrate love, so it was easy for me to believe that what my stepfather offered was love. I had no frame of reference to know that not only was this NOT love but that it was inordinate. I had a father who didn't love me, and a stepfather who loved me inappropriately. As a result, my teenage and young adult years were slathered with inappropriate displays of what I thought love was.

How do you forgive something so overwhelmingly unforgivable? It is impossible without the supernatural power of the Holy Spirit. Please know that forgiveness is indeed a supernatural gift. To be able to forgive someone of an offense that has taken some strong people out is major!!! I spent 40 years believing my father didn't love me. But it took me until I was 45 before I realized it wasn't that he didn't love me…but that he had a mental disorder as a result of the war. He came home from Vietnam with an anti-social personality disorder, PTSD, and he was clinically depressed. I thought he didn't like ME, when in fact, he just didn't like people in general. And now, I am his caregiver, demonstrating and teaching him what real love looks like (by the supernatural power of the Holy Spirit). My father was incapable of showing me what love looked like because of his mental condition, and as a result, I was his collateral damage. As for my stepfather, God made it so that I would cross paths with him one weekday morning some 10+ years after he molested me. I spotted him a ways off. By the time I got to him I was able to hug him and gift him forgiveness. I got on the MetroBus and never saw him again. That act of forgiveness was instant and without residue. That experience was no longer a trigger in my life, and I no longer held the negative feelings for him in my heart.

I know the source of the power of forgiveness. If I didn't know God, I wouldn't have the capacity to be my father's caretaker, nor would I have been able to forgive my stepfather. Life will best us and make us feel like we cannot forgive offenses against us. The inability to forgive is not because we don't understand what it takes, but because we mistakenly believe that the power to forgive lies within us. It has NOTHING to do with us or our personality…REAL forgiveness is supernatural, and it's all a result of the power of God present in our lives.

I never felt the love of my father because he was incapable of giving it to me. My stepfather made me the victim of child molestation. But forgiveness made me the victor and no longer his victim. The weapons formed, but they did not prosper. They made me stronger and helped shape me into who I am today. Somebody tell the devil...I Made It Anyway!!!

Use

What is in

Your Hand

By Jackey Jackson

Success should be measured by your obedience to God, not measured by man. This is a story of how life looks when the Lord tells you to use what is in your hand.

Have you ever had something that you worked so hard for taken away? I started out as a realtor for what I thought were personal reasons. I purchased my first home as a single mom at the age of 23. I knew nothing about the process before, during, or after but I had my keys. A few years later, after purchasing the house, I had a desire to own a 4 unit building. Then, I became interested in real estate investments. I pursued all of these with some degree of success; or, so I thought. And then, things changed. I lost my home to foreclosure due to poor choices and bad money decisions. After I finished waddling in my sorrow I decided that I would one day purchase again but this time it would be different. I would see so many night-time real estate investing programs and I had so many friends looking for homes to rent, I knew there had to be something to this thing called real estate. I also knew that if I could purchase a home as a 23-year-old single mom that I had to get others on board with owning and I had to help them.

All of this was a dream of mine before I had my real estate license. The foreclosure could have killed that dream, but it didn't. I made the decision to take the real estate licensing class as a way to start learning the industry to help others. I affiliated with several companies over the years, trying to find my way in the industry. I've worked with companies from all sizes: big household names hoping it would bring the business, a community-based office to help against predatory lending, and smaller offices hoping for more hands-on help. I was trying to find my way. Have you ever experienced that? You know you're on the right path, but you have to walk it out to find your place. I kept telling myself don't give up. Learn what you can here and keep it moving. But it was hard to stay focused and apply what I learned, in order to sell homes on a consistent basis. The responsibilities of being a single mother and a caregiver to my dad were my top priorities and took up a great deal of my time. I also had the obligations and demands from my "nine to five" which I could not ignore because I relied on that check every two weeks! I know every woman who has made that journey from direct deposits can identify with my struggle here. Nevertheless, my desire to hone my craft as a real estate entrepreneur was also calling me. Pushing me. Driving me forward. Giving me the courage, I needed to keep going.

Let's fast forward some years later, the real estate company my license is with is closing and I have to find a new company to affiliate with. This is where I say, all things work together and you have to walk by faith and not by sight because God knows what is ahead of you. I selected a company to hang my license because I did not want to be considered inactive and unable to do business. However, still working a nine to five and now caregiving for my mom, my nine to five sells the company to a new owner that does not desire to keep any staff. I was a little shaken, but the entrepreneur in me was not destroyed. Entrepreneurs are problem solvers. Have you ever taken the easy way out? Problem solved: file for unemployment and start my job search. Well a few months in just long enough to rest a little, a colleague of mine referred me to a company, I interviewed and was hired on the spot. A year in I heard a similar statement, this time it goes we lost our biggest contract so we will have to downsize. You know the drill last hired first fired. I cried out to God! "What is going on?!?!?"

Well, who would guess that the first company (new owner) calls me and offers me, my old position. Hum, do not get too happy because approximately 4 months in the owner closes the office altogether. As much as I wanted to be mad, I found myself back at God crying out again, "What really is going on??" I must admit while I was at the second company, I felt that I needed to be doing something different, something more.

Now keep in mind I transferred my license because the office closed not because I was going to be a full-time realtor or at least that's what I thought. Well now that I'm unemployed again for the third time in less than two years, I hear the Lord loud and clear, you have a real estate license. I'm feeling that this is the answer to the I need to be doing something different feeling I was having. This is where I would tell you if you have a desire to be an entrepreneur, your business is probably already in your hand.

This is the part where you have to know what you know! You MUST KNOW that God called you to do something or pushed you in a certain direction. Why? Because obstacles or setbacks are a part of the journey.

It wasn't until then that I began to get up every single day with the spirit of an entrepreneur. Although I had my license for years, this would be the first time that I would actually be diving in as a full-time Realtor/ Entrepreneur. The first time I would be solely reliant on myself for income. A tough decision but one I don't regret. Although I was excited I must admit fear of the unknown was real. Have you ever felt that way? Here is where the learning began, and there were many, many questions. Do not be afraid to ask questions, someone in your industry will be willing to share. I remember sitting down with one of the seasoned agents to get an idea of what I should be doing. His question was how can I help you/what questions do you have. The only answer I had was "I don't know what I don't know so tell me anything about starting the business that you think I should know". See what I realized was that there was so much about doing this thing successfully that was not taught in real estate school. See in real estate school you get contract procedures and real estate information. However, they do not tell you how to run a business. They didn't tell me that in addition to showing homes I would be the CEO, CFO, COO, and any other position that needed to be filled. No one warned me that in real estate I had to market myself,

I had to go and secure my next client. I would not sit at a desk while buyers and sellers find me.

At this current office, I was blessed to connect with two powerhouses in the industry that were gifted in making sure that realtors understood that they could sell homes, create a business, and grow their business. This is where I would say you have to watch who you connect with. See connecting to these two placed me in an environment to create my own business and grow it from the ground up. Your foundation has to be solid. Where do you start? I'm glad you asked? My experience taught me that you need, a vision and mission statement, goals, budget, a written plan, and most importantly a mindset of determination. Now in all honesty my first few years none of those things were clearly stated because it was all seemed so overwhelming. Going into my third year it was becoming obvious to me that in addition to the above, systems would be extremely important.

Let us talk about the "M" word, motivation, sometimes referred to as your "Big Why". After a few years of writing my "Big Why" I discovered that most days it did not motivate me or at least not the way I was told it would. I struggled with what do you do when motivation is not kicking you into 3rd or 4th gear or some days not even into 1st gear. For some people this works, but for not for me. I struggled, and the struggle worked against me. How do you stay motivated? I had to realize that it was easier to disregard being motivated and work on being disciplined. Discipline in the actions that would get me the successful results I desired.

We talk about profiles to help us with our clients, but I had to learn me and my nature. I also had to work through my negative thoughts about sales people, and assuming that my potential clients felt the same way. After two years, I still had not reached my goal. I knew I had to continue my work *on me.* I decided that I needed a transformation coach to help me with the internal issues I was feeling and dealing with. I learned that sometimes fear is not just being afraid of the now but sometimes the future success. I learned that my personality would work better for a certain niche of people more than others. I learned that I had to embrace the lovely me God created and not compare it to my colleagues that appeared to have it going on. Most importantly the transformation coaching helped me to see so much about myself that was working against me. Do you ever wonder why you repeat certain behaviors or respond a certain way? Transformation coaching helped me to dig deep and connect some dots from my past. I was able to release some things, forgive some people and most importantly free ME to be able to move freely as I navigate entrepreneurship.

For so long I was told ladies are seen and not heard, or I was used to being in environments where people talked to me, but I wasn't really a part of the conversation. My voice was silenced and I hid behind being an introvert, because people would not expect me to do a lot of talking. But I realized that my not talking to people was not so much that I was afraid to hear no, I've heard no a lot in my life, but it was because I identified with being an introvert, although I enjoyed being around and talking to people. I was often the listener in conversations; I did not know how to hold a conversation that I lead. I wasn't always prepared with the next question in order to make the proper connection to stay in touch with future potential clients. See growing up, I was talked to, I responded and the conversation was over. To grow my business I would have to ask enough good questions then follow up, follow up and follow up again, and for a non-talker that can be draining unless you can make it fun. My old me that I can say now was people-pleasing and passive. For example "Jackey where do you want to eat?" My response was always it doesn't matter, I'm sure I can find something I like on the menu. I know small right but that is my attitude to most things because I always want to make sure those in my presence are happy. Now in customer service that is a good thing, you want your clients' satisfied. However, when it comes to running my business it is not always the case. So not being passive has helped me to ask more good questions and be okay with saying the truth. I'm not sure if this is you, but I was hiding behind being passive by being a people pleaser, is that you? Or perhaps you find yourself always putting others first. Or maybe you avoid the truth to keep from anyone feeling uncomfortable.

In growing your business before you can be service-based you have to be relationship-based because people are your business. Do yourself a favor and have a set of questions that you can ask those you come in contact with to see if they are a good fit for you to work with. Don't waste your God-given time unnecessarily with people and places that will not give you a return. Ask the right questions and remember your clients are trusting you, so ask permission to tell the truth even if they may not agree.

The old me felt rejected early on in life and into my early adult life, so I had to learn to be okay with not getting business from family and friends because that childhood rejection feeling wanted to spill over into my business. I had to learn not to take it personally and remember God had clients assigned to me. I would have to put in the work to find them.

God used a few good leaders in the industry, my coaches and my mentors, to help me connect the dots. I don't know if you have ever had to do this, but I had to take a minute and go a few steps backward to be able to free myself to go forward. Over the last five years of me working as a full-time realtor, I have not met the goals measured by man, but I am pleased to say that each year my income has increased and my understanding of myself has strengthened. I am pleased to say I learned to write a business plan and prepare a budget. I've learned the importance of retreating in October/November to plan for the upcoming year. I've learned that while I am building my business, I am still a wife, mom, caregiver, and community volunteer so managing/prioritizing my time is important. I've learned that I grow as I learn so the importance of connecting with others more experienced, taking classes, reading and webinars are essential. I learned not to ever, ever, *ever* compare my insides to others outside. But most importantly I've learned that while I have goals for my business, God's plan will prevail.

And that's my message to you. If you have a dream, go for it. If you want to start your business and transition from a job-connected paycheck don't let anyone hinder you not even yourself. Allow your God-given passion to make room for you and provide revenue for you.

My Struggle Strengthened Me

*How Verbal Abuse and a
Failed Marriage Pushed Me to My Purpose*

By Minister Tonia King

*Have you ever felt rejected?

*Have you ever felt low and worthless?

*Have you ever felt like you are supposed to be treated in such a way that is unseemly, unjust and unfair?

A Life of Verbal Abuse

I want to share a powerful yet touching story of how my life has been from teenage years until about 30 years old. It wasn't until the age of 30 that I found out that I didn't have to live in a world where people called me any and everything but my birth name. I never had anyone to tell me that God had powerful and loving names for me.

From the age of 12 years old I have dealt with verbal abuse. From relationship to relationship being dating relationships, friends and even associate relationships, I felt like I had to be liked, seeking approval that I allowed others who spoke out of their mouth verbally that they loved me but their actions showed differently. Throughout my life I allowed people to treat me as if I had no value or self-morals.

Have you ever done that? Have you ever wondered why abuse and mistreatment continue to show up in your life? Different people, same pattern! There was a guy in my life that I allowed to control me and run me up and down like a yoyo. As I reflected on my life back then, the guy was so handsome with that wavy hair and those sideburns that made me quiver at the first sight because he kept a fresh haircut which almost seem like he had a live in barber and he smelled so good like he drenched the whole bottle of oil on his clothes. That was a weakness for me. Every time I was in his presence, around people or alone, he would talk to me in a derogatory manner as if I was the bottom of his shoe.

I listened to him telling me that he loved me but after one year of dealing with the verbal abuse and feeling worthless as if I wasn't needed and valued, I felt as if I was supposed to be treated this way. I grew up in church and heard many preachers talk about Psalm 139 which tells me that I'm *fearfully and wonderfully made*. But I didn't believe any of it, because I had never seen it in my life! So many of the people in relationships I was in failed to treat me this way.

I remained in the relationship for one year which felt like eternity. Then, God reminded me of who I was and that I can have everything that pertains to Life and Godliness. I had to muster up enough strength to tell him that it was over. Even though he walked away many times before, this time he left me with a broken heart that tormented me. The spirit of rejection and sense of unworthiness consumed me. It was over when I gave the benediction to the spirit of torment, the spirit of being depressed and rejected by remembering what God said about me.

I want to help someone who is reading this to come to know who you are and to know what you deserve. God called you wonderful, marvelous, and he called you his own. Isaiah 43:11 says I have called you by name and you are mine. **You Can Make It Anyway.** I've listed a few questions at the beginning of this story for you to answer as it will help with your struggle and my hope is that you will allow your responses to strengthen you.

A Failed Marriage

I can only tell you what I experienced; it is important to allow God to order your steps. When we consult God in even the simplest things, he protects us from danger seen and unseen. I know you feel like you should not have to ask God what grocery store you should go to or what exit to take on the beltway but I admonish you that when you ask God and seek him for direction he will lead and guide you. 1 Corinthians 1:27 tells me that he will take the foolish things to confound the wise. During my time of marriage, I felt like I was worthless and existing and not living. I felt like my life had no meaning and I tried to end my life four times because

I felt like life was better dead than alive. It wasn't until I was all out of options of trying to figure out why my marriage was failing and what lessons I needed to learn. Later, I had to admit that my marriage was shaky because I gave more of me and less of God. I had to realize that even though I went through rejection in my early years and I had been delivered I felt like the spirit of rejection and low self-esteem was trying to follow me. This caused me to feel like anything that I draw close to my heart was doomed to fail because I wasn't even happy with myself and I gave God time when I had time. It took me years to realize that even in the marriage I had to take responsibility for putting my trust in a man and trusting that a man will make me happy. I had to learn to lift Jesus up as the bible tells us in John 12:32 that if I be lifted up from the earth I'll draw all men unto me. If you have experienced a failed marriage and if you are like me, you feel like everything that happened was not all your fault and maybe it wasn't but let me help you to understand that you don't have to feel that you can't conquer and soar. Trials come to make you strong and you can live through it. I learned that I can live without apologies and you should know that it's ok to want to feel important, to feel needed and feel worthy. I stand today as an overcomer and I'm grateful for many that prayed for my strength during the struggle. Life is better because of God and if your story is like mine or you have experienced a "Failed Marriage", Stand Up, applaud yourself because the struggle that was intended to break you, gave you strength.

Whether your journey has been rejection, verbal abuse, or divorce; a relationship with Jesus Christ will help to transform your pain to purpose. I know from personal experience that suffering with the pain of low self-esteem and rejection doesn't feel good. In fact it makes you feel Bruised and Battered but I promise you if you give it to Jesus you will discover how to correct your thinking and view of yourself, so that no one else can ever make you doubt your worth again. Don't go off, don't retaliate, and don't give them a piece of your mind! Just ask the Lord to bring you out and you will be able to look back years from now and see where the Lord has brought you from. Like me, your testimony will be "**I MADE IT ANYWAY.**" Your struggle will not destroy you, it will strengthen you.

God Has Been Creating My Puzzle Piece by Piece

By Sandra Scruggs

My life journey began at an early age in a small town, Metcalfe, MS, which would lead me on a discovery of finding Sandra's life purpose and reason for being. I was adopted by my 70-year-old grandmother who raised me and my cousins to the best of her ability. I am so thankful for the knowledge she shared in the short time she raised me. As her health declined, I went to stay with my mother, siblings, and verbally abusive stepfather. Living with my mother was quite different from what I was used to. Living with my grandmother was a loving and warm environment, where my cousins and other siblings wanted to be. She always made us feel that we belonged in this world and had a purpose for being here. As far as I can remember we went to church and learned how to pray. She taught me that God brought you here for a reason and if you look to him and his word, he will carry you through. Being at my mother's house was the complete opposite. I found myself looking for the attention and love that I received from my grandmother's house while living with my mother. My grandmother's house was warm, loving, and felt like a safe space. I enjoyed being with my grandmother, her granddaughter-in-law, along with a host of friends, aunts/uncles that were there to help her take care of me (it truly takes a village). I loved being with my mother and siblings also but knew it was not a stable environment. Seeing my mother and siblings experience that in their household, I knew even at a young age that that is not what I wanted out of life. The confirmation happened when I was sexually assaulted and almost killed in front of family members and had no one there to comfort me. From that moment I found myself looking for love or what I thought was love. The lack of a home parenting life can sometimes change your whole outlook on what life should be.

I became pregnant and delivered my first son when I was just 14 years old, my only daughter at 16, my second son at 18, and my last son at the age of 21. Having 3 kids as a teenager is a struggle. Not knowing how you are going to feed and clothe your children, is very stressful. These are simple necessities that you should be able to provide, not to mention the challenges of putting a roof over your little one's head. Some will look at you and judge and some will try to be helpful. To become a homeless teenager living in a shelter and on government assistance and not knowing which direction to go can be overwhelming. But when you want better for your kids, every fiber in you will motivate you to become better in life, believe in yourself, and have a support system that will be there no matter how bad things get. Meditating on God's word and taking care of your mental health are so important to becoming a better you. Do not feel bad or crazy to seek out help from a good therapist; that's God's purpose and calling for them. They reach out to help others to become a better images of themselves. Nobody knows your true struggle but you and God. And having family and true friends that will support you and be there for you no matter your circumstances is also helpful.

In spite of it all, God had something awesome in store for me. All through my struggles, he had listened to my silent tears and heart-wrenching prayers. It is never too late for God to show up and bless you! When I was 20 years old, and a single mother of three children, a wonderful man came into my life. This man of faith became my everything, after we met through a mutual friend and coworker. That is when I had to really dig deep and find Sandra. I began going to church, reading the word, trying to figure out my life and what I wanted to become. After losing my job and soul searching what I wanted out of life for myself and my family, I told my husband/fiancé at the time I wanted to open a family child care center to be able to help young mothers that needed help caring for their kids. I wanted to have additional income to support my children. I did not want my daughter to become another teenage mother statistic. Also, raising 3 African American boys is already challenging in America. I wanted to provide so they wouldn't be out in the streets or worse, in the prison system. So, I started taking classes and continued my education on how to open a successful family childcare business. I also wanted to give parents that secure feeling *of "I can leave my child and go to work/ school without worrying about my child's needs. I feel comfortable leaving my child in an environment built on learning and love."* This is why I give my all to provide the best experience in a family childcare setting. I just did not want any parent or anyone to experience what I went through as a teenage and adult looking for that trustworthy caregiver. After my first year, I had become a successful entrepreneur in the family childcare business in that time I was able to meet early childhood educators that I now consider as friends and family. This business has given my family so many blessings and advantages. The business put all four of our kids through college, something that I never would have thought of in my wildest dreams, but God kept providing.

Along my journey, I have been able to connect with amazing people from all walks of life. I have also encountered people that stirred up my emotions and provoked me to become detached from God and his plan for my life. These experiences forced me to become a better person and mother to my children. I watched my oldest son pursue his motivational career while obtaining a degree in accounting. I have seen my daughter raise her two sons while becoming a hairstylist and an entrepreneur. I have been able to see every game my two youngest sons have played on national TV, during Saturday college football games. I was extremely proud when one of my sons received an opportunity to play for the NFL. He applied that same determination and drive to being a father. And, and as a mother, nothing makes me happier.

Who would have thought my life could be this way? But those experiences taught me how to navigate through life and continue to find myself and be a wife which nobody tells you when you get married what to expect. Growing up, I did not see that side of love and passion until later in life and then there is an aha moment. My husband has also been my biggest supporter and there are not enough words to describe how much I love and appreciate him for loving me. I can honestly say he is my knight and shining armor. If God did it for me, He will do the same thing for you.

But then the kids go off to school and it is a whole new world when they become adults. Then it becomes all about you. Everything comes at you full circle. Now my husband and I are focusing our time to find our purpose because we were focused on the kids. What were my other goals in life? Let us go back to school, take some educational courses, go get a massage, read a book, arts and crafts. I started my notary business. I became a travel agent, because I love going new places and seeing the world. But my passion will always be trying to bring family and people together to just celebrate life and have a great time in the presence of others while still putting yourself first. Whatever your passion or purpose is, seek it out and find yourself. I have been investing in self-love and lots of self care, reading my bible, daily devotionals, and becoming a Proverbs 31 Woman which gives me so much power, purpose, and success in life, while using my God given talents. Never let anyone steal that away from you. Follow God's guidance; it will lead you all the way to the Promised Land. There are still pieces to my puzzle, but God is my glue to my pain, purpose, passion, and power.

No More Apologies

By Pastor Veda A. McCoy

The year was 1990, I was six months pregnant with my daughter, Johntae. At dinner one Sunday evening, a friend told me that she was going back to school. I took note, because I had wanted to go back to school for several years, since graduating from high school six years prior in 1984. In my mind, I thought, "You should be back in school. You should be finished by now." This dialogue was typical self-talk for me. I had developed a very critical inner voice, judging and condemning myself for all of the things I should have done by now. And in my opinion, the list was long.

I could not figure out how my life had gotten so off track. I was supposed to "do so much." In school, I took honors and TAG classes. In high school, I took AP English and scored high enough on the exit exam to test out of two semesters of freshman literature. I was a track star who still held high school records. My girls track team was a force at the high school, district, regional and state levels. We ran in the 4x100 finals heat at Penn Relays. I still have that medal somewhere. I had gotten academic and athletic scholarships to two Virginia universities. But here I was poor – *really poor!* My husband and I were more like P-O ~ Po! And, I was pregnant with my second child, at 23 years old. I was working at a job that paid the bills, but it did not have much promotion or growth potential. It certainly did not measure up to what I had envisioned for myself. I was definitely under-achieving in life.

All of this weighed heavily on me even more, for some reason, after that Sunday dinner with friends. Somehow, hearing that someone else who was young, married and a mother was going back to school, motivated me to do the same. So, with a baby in my big belly, I went to the University of District Columbia, and I enrolled. It was the summer time, extremely hot and humid, but I didn't care. It was time for me to get my life back on track. But taking outward actions does not mean that your inner work is complete. This was true of me as well; nevertheless, I was on my way without even really knowing it. Life has a way of bringing you face to face with your issues, so that you can no longer avoid or run away from them.

While at UDC, I met two professors who changed my life, probably without even knowing it. One was a female English professor with fair skin, jet black wavy hair, and piercing blue eyes. I thought she was beautiful. The other was a philosophy professor. He was distinguished, articulate and very poised. He reminded me Supreme Court Justice Thurgood Marshall. From the very first lectures, I was mesmerized by her undeniable good looks and his captivating intellect. Brilliance and Beauty. Two things I desired for myself. Two things I did not realize I already had. I have always been an inquisitive person, so I tend to ask a lot of questions. I asked the philosophy professor, "How do you know when you are smart enough and have enough education to succeed." He responded, "When you realize you don't know everything and will NEVER know everything." And then he said something that totally blew my mind. He said to me, "The fact that you asked that question, proves that you're already pretty smart. Young lady, you're not here because you're not smart. You are one of the more brilliant students I've met in a long time." I looked around to see whom he was really talking to. Certainly not me! The one who got married the year after high school and had a son a year later, at just 19 years old. I clearly wasn't getting it, so the lessons continued. I asked my English professor, "How does it feel to be so pretty, to have the looks that everybody wants." She responded, "Actually, I don't feel "lucky" or "blessed" about my looks at all, because I don't I don't fit in everywhere. Truthfully, my looks cause me to be rejected by both groups of people. Black people reject me because they resent the advantages they think my looks get me. But, they still don't think I'm black enough. White people reject me because my looks remind them of truths they'd rather forget. But yet, I'm still not white enough to be one of them." And then SHE said something that shook me up as well. She said, "But, Veda, *you are* beautiful. You have amazing facial features and beautiful smooth, brown skin. Never doubt that." Now I knew she was tripping or feeling sorry for me or something. I had always had issues with my looks. To me, my dark skin, thick hips and kinky hair were anything but beautiful. Even though I didn't believe them initially, I knew deep down inside that they were telling me what they believed to be true. And, while it would take me a while to really step into the truth of what they tried share with me, it was a start. It was definitely a life changing moment. I would not finish school for another nine years, fifteen years after graduating from high school. And I still struggle from time to time with a very critical inner voice, but that time in my life changed everything. I stopped apologizing for what I had not done and who I had not become. And, I focused on being and doing my best.

These two people were essentially strangers to me, but they taught me a valuable lesson. Validation and self-worth had to come from within. I had to believe that I was good enough, smart enough, and beautiful enough. I was ENOUGH, and I had what it took to pursue my passions, fulfill my purpose and reach my destiny. I continued at UDC for a few years, still trying to juggle being a young wife, mother, working full time, being in full time ministry, and finding myself – all at the same time. In 1997, I transferred to Bowie State University and graduated in December, 1999, magna cum laude. In January 2000, I left my job as a legal secretary, took at $32,000 pay cut to begin my career as an educator, starting out as a substitute teacher. Twenty-two years later, I have two master degrees – one in Education and one in Theology. I am a dissertation away from my doctorate degree in Educational Leadership. I am a career educator with a wonderful network of colleagues who love, respect and support me. Seven years ago, I became the Principal of an elementary school. I have recorded and released three solo CDs and travelled the world with many gospel greats, including The Winans and Pastor Shirley Caesar. In 2004, my husband and I started a church and we've pastored together successfully, for seventeen years. And, I am an international speaker, spiritual coach, mentor and author. I am also a *Purpose Pusher* for women, helping as many as I can to walk in their purpose.

I don't have many regrets, because I really believe that are no failures in life. There are only lessons. But one regret I must admit to having is that I did not realize how awesome and amazing I was until way too late in my life. That's right! You've got to know your worth and value. You've got to know WHO you are and WHOSE you are. You can't really show up for others in a true and meaningful way, until you know who it is that you are trying to show up to be. If I had to give you one bit of advice it would be to learn and embrace this truth, as early as possible. I went back to college to "finally get my life together" and to "finally finish school." But God had other things in store for me. He wanted me to truly know, Psalm 139:14, *I will give thanks unto thee; for I am fearfully and wonderfully made: Wonderful are thy works; and that my soul knows right well.* (ASV). When your soul knows how precious you are to God, the rest of your life will show it. That's the best praise you can give God, to show forth the glory that is revealed in you, His creation. So, make no apologies for your journey. Make no apologies for the lessons you've had to learn. They've all been dress rehearsals for your "main stage" performance in your next dimension of life.

Pastor Veda A. McCoy

Pastor Veda is an international speaker, spiritual coach, author and singer who helps women to unlock their purpose, power and prosperity, through the pursuit of their passion. Known as "the Purpose Guru" - PURPOSE PROFICIENCY is Pastor Veda's passion. She has coached and mentoring thousands of women through retreats, conferences, seminars and empowering programs, including *SOLitude Women's Retreat, Dreams Unlocked, I Am Esther Coaching and Mentoring Program Passion of Esther Mentoring Program, Finding Elizabeth Mentoring Training Program, the Annual Prophetic Prayer Breakfast,* and, most recently, *Exhale Virtual Experience for Women.*

Pastor Veda teaches women how to leverage their purpose into streams of income, generating financial freedom and increasing their capacity to build a legacy of impact and service. As they climb the ladder of success, she provides spiritually based strategies to keep them grounded while they **"operate in their purpose on purpose."**

Pastor Veda is the recipient of the *Let Freedom Ring" Outstanding Educator's Award,* presented by Rev. Jesse L. Jackson, Sr. and The PUSH Coalition, and the Trailblazer's Award, from the SoulWeath® Foundation for Women.

She is a career educator and has worked for over 20 years in Prince George's County Public Schools. Starting as a substitute teacher, she is now an elementary school principal. She has over 35 years of corporate and religious experience, which allows her to bring messages right to her listener's heart.

Since 2004, Veda McCoy has served as the Executive Pastor of Judah Christian Center, in Clinton, MD, a church she founded with her husband, Overseer Marvin E. McCoy. A strong believer in faith-based community leadership, Pastor Veda works closely with the Prince George's County Faith Based Advisory. Through this partnership, she coordinated the Be Inspired Virtual Conference for Educators, to help teachers navigate the distance learning environment. Since June 2020, Pastor Veda has served on the organization's Committee on Education, where she facilitates a monthly check-in for parents and produces a newsletter with information and resources to help families navigate distance learning.

Follow Pastor Veda on Social Media

www.vedamccoy.com

Facebook and IG @IAmVedaMcCoy

LinkedIn and Twitter @vedamccoy

Join Pastor Veda for the

Exhale Virtual Experience for Women

January 7 – 8, 2022

Register at Exhale2022.eventbrite.com

Made in the USA
Middletown, DE
15 April 2021

37702138R00024